The Library of the Civil Rights Movement™

The Little Rock Nine

Young Champions for School Integration

Jake Miller

The Rosen Publishing Group's

PowerKids Press™

New York

Published in 2004 by The Rosen Publishing Group, Inc.
29 East 21st Street, New York, NY 10010

First Edition

Editor: Frances E. Ruffin
Book Design: Emily Muschinske

Photo Credits: Cover and title page, pp. 5, 8 (far right), 10, 15, 16, 19, 20 © Bettmann/CORBIS, pp. 6, 8 (top left), 11 (inset) © Library of Congress, Prints and Photographs Division; p. 8 © AP/Wide World; pp. 11, 12 © Frances Miller/Timepix.

Miller, Jake, 1969–
The Little Rock Nine : young champions for school integration / Jake Miller.— 1st ed.
   p. cm. — (The library of the civil rights movement)
Includes bibliographical references (p.) and index.
  ISBN 0–8239–6252–0 (library binding)
1. School integration—Arkansas—Little Rock—History—20th century—Juvenile literature. 2. African American students—Arkansas—Little Rock—History—20th century—Juvenile literature. 3. Central High School (Little Rock, Ark.)—History—Juvenile literature. 4. Little Rock (Ark.)—Race relations—Juvenile literature. [1. School integration—Arkansas—History. 2. African Americans—Civil rights—History. 3. Little Rock (Ark.)—Race relations.] I. Title.
  LC214.23.L56 M55 2003
  379.2'63'0976773—dc21

2001007241

Manufactured in the United States of America

Contents

Students and Soldiers

Even on a normal day, Central High School in Little Rock, Arkansas, looks like a **fortress**. It is five stories high, two blocks long, and one block deep. It has towering brick walls and stone towers. For nine black students on September 4, 1957, Central High looked like a battle zone. Rows and rows of armed soldiers surrounded the school. They weren't there to protect the school from an invading army. They were there to make sure that nine recently **enrolled** students did not enter the building. Those nine students were supposed to be the first black children to attend all-white Central High. However, that morning in September, soldiers from Arkansas's national guard, along with a mob of white **protesters**, were determined to keep the black students out of the school.

Elizabeth Eckford, right and inset, attempted to enter Central High School, but she was prevented from entering by armed troops who were placed in front of the school to keep black students out.

Then and Now

In 1957, Arkansas governor Orval Faubus was determined to keep Little Rock schools segregated. In 1997, former Arkansas governor and U.S. president Bill Clinton honored the Little Rock Nine for their courage in integrating Central High School.

The Little Rock Nine

It took incredible bravery and **determination** for the nine black students to face the mob of angry white people. Central High had 2,000 white students. It was the best high school in Little Rock and one of the best in the nation. The black students knew that going there would help them get into good colleges. The nine students were chosen for their excellent grades, but they also had parents who encouraged them to face the tough battle ahead. The students' names were Minnijean Brown, Elizabeth Eckford, Ernest Green, Thelma Mothershed, Melba Pattillo, Gloria Ray, Terrence Roberts, Jefferson Thomas, and Carlotta Walls. The struggle of these black students to **integrate** Central High was an important story. Reporters from around the world came to Little Rock to write about them.

The nine black students who integrated Central High School soon became known around the world as the Little Rock Nine, or the Nine. This photograph shows them with Daisy Bates (inset), a local journalist.

A Plan for Integration

The struggle to **desegregate** Central High began in May 1955, one year after the U.S. Supreme Court issued a decision in the famous case of *Brown v. Board of Education of Topeka*. The court's decision made it illegal to **segregate** black and white students and to have them attend separate schools. Schools in Arkansas were beginning to change to follow the law. The nearby town of Hoxie, Arkansas, integrated its schools in 1955. Little Rock was under order from a federal judge to integrate, too. Daisy Bates, a black woman who was a local civil rights **activist** and **journalist**, worked with the school board for more than one year on plans to integrate Little Rock's schools. Their three-step plan would first integrate the senior high schools, then the junior high schools, and, finally, the elementary schools.

Left: *Daisy Bates helped the Nine enter Central High.* Middle: *In 1954, Thurgood Marshall,* (the man in the middle) *had won a Supreme Court case to integrate schools.* Right: *This sign belonged to segregationists.*

Governor Orval Faubus

Orval Faubus, the governor of Arkansas, was facing reelection in 1958. Many of Arkansas's white voters hated the idea of integration and were angry that the Supreme Court and the national government had told their local schools what to do. Faubus wanted to prove to **racist** voters that he was a tough supporter of segregation. On September 2, 1957, just two days before schools in Little Rock were to open, Faubus went on television. Faubus declared Central High off-limits to blacks. He warned that "blood would run in the streets" if they didn't keep away. **White supremacists** from all over Arkansas were gathering in Little Rock to protest desegregation.

Orval Faubus ordered the Arkansas National Guard to prevent black students from entering Central High School. Inset: The sign Faubus holds states that he is against integration in Little Rock.

AGAINST RACIAL INTEGRATION OF ALL SCHOOLS WITHIN THE LITTLE ROCK SCHOOL DISTRICT.... ☐

A Scary First Day of School

On September 4, 1952, Daisy Bates had planned to meet the nine black students and a group of local ministers at a corner near Central High. They would all try to enter the school together. Only eight of the students heard about the plan. Elizabeth Eckford did not have a telephone at home and never got the message. The group made its way through the crowds and was turned away by the national guardsmen. When Elizabeth tried to enter the school from the opposite side, she soon became surrounded by protesters calling her names and threatening her. With the help of a *New York Times* reporter and the wife of a local professor, Elizabeth got onto a bus and made it to safety.

Elizabeth Eckford leaves Central High School, trailed by white protesters. The reporter who helped Elizabeth get away safely told her, "Don't let them see you cry."

National Guard Sent Home

As the first weeks of September went by, U.S. president Dwight Eisenhower was starting to get worried. Governor Faubus openly **defied** federal law. Faubus met with Eisenhower and agreed to follow the court order to allow integration. Faubus promised that he would order national guard troops to protect the nine students from the mobs. Instead, on September 23, he sent the troops home. With a small force of Little Rock police officers to protect them, the Nine snuck into Central High. They used a side entrance to avoid the mob of protesters. Meanwhile, the mob attacked reporters who had gathered to cover the story. The police chief decided that, with only a few police officers to protect them, it was too dangerous to let the Nine stay in school. He sent them home.

In this picture, four of the Little Rock Nine students try to enter Central High School, but a mob of white students and adults insult them and prevent them from entering.

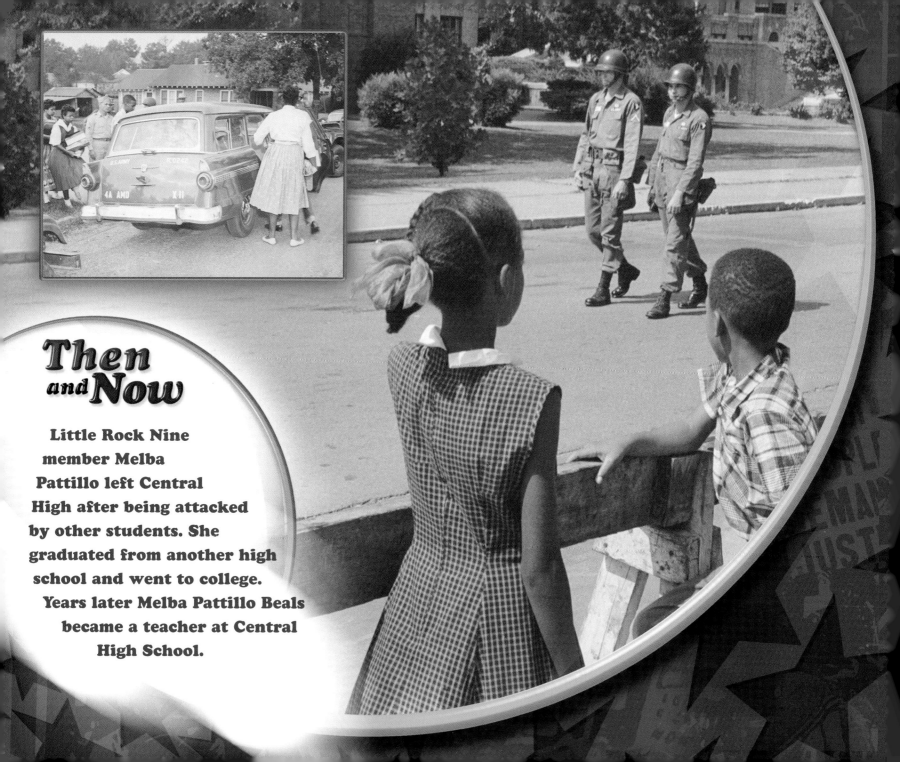

Then and Now

Little Rock Nine member Melba Pattillo left Central High after being attacked by other students. She graduated from another high school and went to college. Years later Melba Pattillo Beals became a teacher at Central High School.

Federal Troops Protect Little Rock Nine

After Orval Faubus sent away the national guard, President Eisenhower decided that he could not trust the authorities in Arkansas to protect the Little Rock Nine. He decided to use federal troops, who would be under his own command. In this way, he could be sure the law would be followed. He called for 1,000 of the best troops in the U.S. Army, the **paratroopers** of the 101st Airborne. They were known as the Screaming Eagles. Eisenhower also placed the Arkansas national guard under federal command, so that they would follow his orders instead of Governor Faubus's. On September 24, 1957, a unit of 350 paratroopers **escorted** the Little Rock Nine into school. It was three weeks into the school year, but they were finally able to attend their first full day of classes.

Little Rock schoolchildren watch paratroopers arrive in their city. Inset: The Little Rock Nine students were driven to school in a U.S. Army station wagon for their protection.

A Tough Time in the School

For two months each of the Nine had a soldier as a personal bodyguard while he or she attended classes. Even though they had guards, the Nine were teased, threatened, and attacked by their fellow students. Melba Pattillo had a stick of **dynamite** with a lit fuse thrown at her. She was also stabbed and had acid sprayed in her eyes. She probably would have gone blind from the acid if the soldier who was guarding her hadn't quickly rinsed her eyes with water. After months of being called names and taking much worse abuse from white students, Minnijean Brown was expelled from school. She had called a white student a name after that student had called her a name. Minnijean was given a second chance, but she was eventually expelled for good. She dumped her cafeteria tray on a group of students who had teased her.

Little Rock Nine students are shown at lunch in the Central High cafeteria. Inset: *A black college student visiting Central High is escorted through an angry crowd.*

The Families Suffered, Too

The Little Rock Nine and their families had problems outside of school. Some of the Nine and their families had to leave town. Their parents were fired by racist bosses, because they had sent their children to a white school. Others just couldn't stand the stress and moved away from Little Rock. Although Daisy Bates was also threatened, she continued to support the students and their parents. She talked with the families about their concerns. She wrote to politicians to try to get them to support integration. She talked to reporters to make sure the story of the Little Rock Nine was told around the world. Only three of the Little Rock Nine remained to graduate from Central High School.

 The Nine were (floor, left to right) Thelma Mothershed, Elizabeth Eckford, Melba Pattillo, *and (above, left to right)* Jefferson Thomas, Ernest Green, Minnijean Brown, Carlotta Walls, Terrence Roberts, *and* Gloria Ray.

Sweet Victories

On May 27, 1958, Ernest Green became the first black student to graduate from Central High. Carlotta Walls graduated in 1959, and Jefferson Thomas graduated in 1960. Although many of them did not remain in Little Rock, each of the Nine went on to earn college degrees. They grew up to be teachers, professors, writers, and powerful bankers. Besides these personal victories, the Little Rock Nine started important changes that affected the whole United States. On Sept 12, 1958, the Supreme Court ruled that every state had to follow the *Brown* ruling to desegregate their schools. It was an important victory for the **Civil Rights movement**. The federal government proved that it was willing to fight for the right of all of its citizens, black and white, to have an equal education.

Glossary

activist (AK-tih-vist) A person who does things like protest and demonstrate to support a cause he or she believes in.

Civil Rights movement (SIH-vul RYTS MOOV-mint) People and groups working together to win freedom and equality for all.

defied (dih-FYD) Refused to obey.

desegregate (dee-SEH-gruh-gayt) To bring divided groups together to end their separation.

determination (dih-ter-meh-NAY-shun) The act of taking a firm stand for a purpose.

dynamite (DY-nuh-myt) A powerful explosive used in blasting rock.

enrolled (en-ROHLD) To have become a student in a school or a member of a group.

escorted (es-KORT-ed) To go along with someone to show respect or to protect that person.

fortress (FOR-tres) A place that can be defended from attack.

integrate (IN-tuh-grayt) To bring different races together to form one group.

journalist (JER-nuhl-ist) A person who gathers, writes, and presents news for television, a newspaper, or a magazine.

paratroopers (PAYR-uh-troo-perz) Soldiers who are trained to jump out of airplanes for combat.

protesters (PROH-tes-terz) People who march or demonstrate for change.

racist (RAY-sist) A person who believes that one group, or race, of people is better than another group.

segregate (SEH-gruh-gayt) To separate people by race or ethnic group.

white supremacists (WYT suh-PREH-muh-sists) People who believe that white people are better than other racial or ethnic groups.

Index

Primary Sources

Cover: A 1957 photograph of the Little Rock Nine. **Page 5:** September 4, 1957 photograph of Elizabeth Eckford being turned away from Central High School by the national guard (1957). **Page 5 (inset):** The national guard troops were withdrawn from Central High School (1957). **Page 6:** The Nine and Daisy Bates. Photograph Cecil Layne. From NAACP records (1957). **Page 8 (center photo):** Attorneys who argued *Brown v. Board*, Hayes, Marshall, and Nabrit in front of U.S. Supreme Court Building (1954). **Page 8 (right):** A sign protesting integration (1959). **Page 11:** The Arkansas national guard keeping black students out of Central High (1957), photograph by Francis Miller 1959. **Page 12:** Elizabeth Eckford, photograph by Francis Miller (1957). **Page 15:** Four black students attempt to enter Central High School (1957). **Page 16 (inset):** The Little Rock Nine going to school in a U.S. Army station wagon (1957). **Page 16:** Black children watch paratroopers arrive at Central High School (1957). **Page 19 (inset):** September 5, 1957 photograph by Bettmann. A black college student visiting Central High School being escorted through an angry crowd (1957). **Page 19:** Jefferson Thomas and Elizabeth Eckford in the lunch room at Central High School (1957). **Page 20:** Little Rock Nine formed a study group when kept out of school (1957).

Web Sites

Due to the changing nature of internet links, PowerKids Press has developed an online list of Web sites related to the subject of this book. This site is updated regularly. Please use this link to access the list.
www.powerkidslinks.com/lcrm/lrnine/